T0197196

BOSS

The Handbook for Anyone Who Has a Boss
or Anyone Who Would Like to be a Boss

JAMES W. ROSE

BALBOA.PRESS

A DIVISION OF HAY HOUSE

Balboa Press books may be ordered through booksellers or by contacting:

Balboa Press
A Division of Hay House
1663 Liberty Drive
Bloomington, IN 47403
www.balboapress.com
844-682-1282

Print information available on the last page.

ISBN: 979-8-7652-3598-0 (sc)
ISBN: 979-8-7652-3600-0 (hc)
ISBN: 979-8-7652-3599-7 (e)

Library of Congress Control Number: 2022920213

Balboa Press rev. date: 11/22/2022

To all the bosses I have worked for,
good or bad:
I have learned a great deal
from each and every one.

Contents

Introduction

How to Use This Book

Boss is a working handbook that you should keep accessible at all times. If you are having trouble with a boss or just want to improve your relationship with your boss, this handbook is a great tool for you. It will help you:

- determine what type of a boss you are dealing with (or if you categorize your boss as a combination of types, see chapter 3);

- review the dos and don'ts of each boss;

- identify the type of environment you are working in;

- make a decision on your plan of attack and establish a goal that you want to achieve;

- organize a plan of achievement focusing on your goal;

- work toward your goal, reviewing your plan regularly and consulting the book throughout the process as needed, and continue until you have achieved your goal;

- further or refine your plan as time goes on.

Good luck!

1

Bosses Categorized

There are many factors that affect how a boss behaves. This book will not be discussing why a boss acts in the manner they do, or how the boss got to where they are. Instead, I will be offering some ways to categorize bosses in order to give some insight on how to negotiate a boss. The book may also give you insight into options should you choose the path of becoming a boss.

A boss does not necessarily fit into just one category. Some categories by nature involve other categories or will lead to other categories. For example, the "green" or inexperienced boss may develop over time into another category. So don't think of a category as binding a boss for life. It is hoped that bosses are trying to develop their skills and will evolve, thus improving as time goes on.

Read through each of the following categories and reflect on the boss you are dealing with—or the kind of boss you would like to be known as.

True Leader

This is the boss everyone dreams of having. This person is a great leader. You feel good when you are around them. You want to work for this boss, and you are motivated to do the best you can.

Egotistical Boss

This is the boss who wants to get all the attention and all the credit. Often the egotistical boss will say what they believe people want to hear, but more than likely, their action will contradict what they say.

Power Boss

The power boss uses their title to force and bully employees to comply. Fear is the ultimate tool for this boss.

The Micromanager

This boss thinks they know everything and therefore tries to take control of everything. The micromanager does not rely on the employees who often know much more in their respective areas than the boss does.

"Nice" Boss

This is the boss everyone says is a "nice guy" or "nice woman." However, this person may not have much knowledge or get much respect in the workplace and often will not be able to get things done.

Green Boss

This is a new boss, and everyone knows it because they make novice mistakes and may lack confidence. In time, this boss will move into another category.

Crazy Boss

Everyone wonders how this boss got to where they are. They are irrational, often not honest, often negative, and usually create problems and issues. You may be shocked at the unreality and the number of lies they develop, all with a purpose of protecting themselves and perhaps trying to ruin the reputation of others. Typically, this person will have other abnormalities that stand out socially or personally.

The Politician

This boss is very similar to the egotistical boss in that they are all about self-gain. They will say things to get support from followers and manipulate facts to meet their needs. But the politician differs from the egotistical boss in that they may not need to be the center of attention. However, they will do anything to make sure their support is strong.

Incompetent Boss

This is a boss who does not belong where they are. This person does not have the skills to be successful. The incompetent boss can become very dangerous and will often do whatever they can to protect themselves and place blame on others.

Motivational Boss

This boss has skills in motivation, and their presence is a positive influence. They are always upbeat and try to empower everyone around them, but they may not actually take part in the work themselves.

Stressed-Out Boss

This is the boss who is always screaming at someone. They have a short fuse. They do not care if they scream at someone in an inappropriate setting or in front of others.

The Nuclear Reactor

This is a boss who reacts to everything—and often the reaction is too much for whatever occurred. However, given a little time, this boss may come back to their senses. The nuclear reactor might be confused with a stressed boss. But the stressed boss is always screaming, while the nuclear reactor boss immediately has an excessive reaction to a situation or problem but given time may come to the right decision. It is important for this boss to realize they are in this category so they can set a pattern of behavior by waiting before making decisions.

Absent Boss

This boss is often not around and is not involved. People wonder how they keep their job because they are never at work. Employees can feel like they are alone on an island without the proper support.

Substance-Abusing Boss

This boss has addiction problems, whether it is alcohol, drugs, or something else. This boss needs help. Addiction is a disease like any other, and without the proper help and support, this medical condition could lead to death. Nonetheless, this boss can put employees in difficult positions with dilemmas about proper conduct, professionalism, loyalty, and safety. The substance-abusing boss is often absent as well.

Average Everyday Boss

This is the typical boss, and one who does not necessarily fit well into any one category. They come into work and do their job. Sometimes you like what they do, and sometimes you do not. You do not have strong feelings one way or the other. Often, they aren't doing any harm, but your institution also won't be receiving any high honors under them.

Insecure Boss

This is a boss with little sense of self-confidence or trust. The insecure boss believes it is important to have their best friends in positions to support them. Often, their friends, relatives, and old colleagues are put into positions even when they do not have the qualifications for the job. The typical first step of this boss is to get rid of anyone who does not meet the criteria.

The Hitman or Hitwoman

This boss is on a mission to get rid of someone. They may be acting on orders from someone above them or under the influence of a misguided colleague—or maybe just on hearsay. The hitman or hitwoman wants their target out and will do anything they can to achieve the goal.

The Manipulator

This is a boss who will twist the truth. This boss will talk behind your back and tries to manipulate employees and colleagues into believing or doing something to the boss's advantage. People are tools to them.

Family Boss

This is the boss in a family-owned business. If you're part of the family, your boss could be your parent, grandparent, an aunt or uncle, or even a sibling. This can be a very good and secure situation but carries its own set of challenges. When things go wrong, there can be lasting effects on the family outside work. And working for a family boss when you are not in the family also has some challenges. It's likely that this boss will also be categorized in another category.

The Best Friend

This boss just wants to be your best friend. A boss who desires friendship may make decisions in an effort to gain it. Difficult discussion may not take place, to avoid straining the relationship. A boss who develops these friendships can cause tensions among workers, such as jealousy or anger, especially in bigger institutions. But a friendship with the boss could make your life easy in a small environment—as long as everything is going well.

The Social Media Boss

This is my newest category, but one that is growing rapidly. This boss lives through social media and tries to control and manipulate the work environment in this way. This form of manipulation is based on the principle that if it is on the web for people to read, it will be read and believed, no matter how false the information may be. The social media boss is often combined with another category.

Interim Boss

The interim boss is only in the position temporarily. Perhaps someone else has already been hired, and this boss is filling in temporarily. Or perhaps the position is being reviewed, and the organization wants to wait a year or so to hire a person on a more permanent basis. But included in this category is the leader who takes a position intending to leave as soon as possible for a better position. Whatever the reason, this person does not have a long-term vision or plan. They will do the minimal to keep things going. Usually this is not a problem for the worker, provided you are doing what you are supposed to be doing. However, this category is often combined with other categories that can make this leader more difficult to deal with.

2

The Dos and Don'ts for Each Type of Boss

Now that you have identified what category or categories your boss fits in, it is time to discuss how to interact with your boss. What can you do? What should you avoid? As you read this chapter, keep in mind that these suggestions are based on the category. You will have to take into account the many other factors that may be personal to you and your situation, the atmosphere you are in, and your work history, as well as your strengths and weaknesses. But I hope that these dos and don'ts will help you decide what will work best for you so that when you reach chapter 4, you'll be ready to make a decision and develop an action plan.

True Leader

This is the boss most everyone wants to work for. You are very motivated to do the best you can for this boss. The true leader wants you to do the best you can and probably has the skills to support you in working better than even you imagined. So make sure you give your 110 percent at all times. Do not be a minimalist or time-watcher. Become part of the team and be positive. You are working for the best, so you need to be the best as well.

Egotistical Boss

You need to understand that it is all about this boss. To stay on the good side of the egotist, you need to feed their ego. However, you should never compromise your character, integrity, and honesty, or you could become a person who may not be viewed in a favorable manner. Often this boss does not have the confidence to support anyone they consider a threat. Never make this person look bad in front of others. Taking small steps to make this boss look good could go a long way in your relationship. You might give the boss some good information, or guide them out of a situation that they may not have been aware of.

Remember, egotistical bosses are focused on themselves and how they look. They are not typically the boss who will go after people, so if you do your job and give them positive support and proper guidance, you should be in good shape.

Power Boss

With this boss, it's all about who is in charge. To stay on their good side, it is important to show that you know they're in charge. Questioning this boss or their authority will bring out the bear in this person. It is their way or the highway. You may need to review the situation often. But remember—and this cannot be repeated too many times—you should never give up your character, integrity, and honesty. You may need to hold back on honesty if it will set off this person in charge; sometimes with this boss, the less said the better. If you are forced to do something that you know will not be good, you will need to make a decision. Be honest and tactful, even though you may have to carry out the task. Sometimes it may be helpful to put the problems in writing, but with this boss it will probably cause more problems with your future.

You may need additional support from a better leader if you have access to one who could help. If not, make sure other employees you trust are aware of the situation. The more people who are aware, the better it will be for you when the end result turns out the way you said it would, because this boss will likely blame you in the end.

The Micromanager

I have to start the dos and don'ts here with one of my favorite quotes for talking about this type of boss: "micromanagement plus ignorance causes failure." If you are the expert in your area and you work for a micromanager who is not, you will be facing a frustrating situation. Here are a few things that might help, since this person wants to be the know-it-all about everything.

This boss usually likes to receive a request for help or a question to answer, which puts them into the role of mentor. However, for this to be successful, it is important to find something that they actually know about. If you find something to ask them about, you will get some "points" for showing them you respect their knowledge and insight. But when you are being micromanaged by someone who does not have the expertise, all you can do is to try to educate them. Since in the micromanager's mind, they already know everything, this education can become very difficult. Tact is called for. Often, you must educate them without letting them know that they are being taught and that you are the one doing it.

If you are cornered, you may need to put the problems in writing, explaining the decision you believe needs to be made, based on your experience, and identifying possible consequences. When this does not work out well, the micromanager is another category of boss who may not take the blame for their own actions.

"Nice" Boss

This boss wants to be liked. Thus this boss will usually not make waves, unless they are called out for not getting much done. To keep the relationship good between you and the "nice" boss, just do your job and try not to get them involved. Do not depend on them, because you may be disappointed. Be nice to them, because they likely will be nice to you. Keep discussions light and do your job.

Green Boss

This category is one you should follow closely. They are learning, and it is likely that everyone knows it. Develop a positive relationship by letting them know you are there for them in whatever capacity they may need. If you are a veteran employee, you can give them valuable information and maybe help them develop into a true leader. The longer you work for this person and guide their development, the more insight you will have into what boss categories they will end up in. Keep a close watch on this boss, as their development can go in many directions.

Crazy Boss

This is perhaps the most challenging boss to work for, because this boss can manifest in many ways. Every day and every contact can be totally different from the one before. The best advice I can give here is to do your job, and document to protect yourself. Document the irrational, unpredictable, or unstable behavior you witness, or any attacks that been inflicted on you and others. Try to stay below the radar. Sometimes in difficult situations, it is important to laugh. It can make you feel better!

You do not have control over the crazy boss's actions, and they often do not have control over their actions. Sometimes the only control is whether they are taking the proper medications.

If the person does last in this position, eventually you may have to make a decision about whether to continue working for them. First learn where this boss is getting the support that is keeping them in the position. This could be helpful information in developing a plan if you decide to stay (chapter 4).

The Politician

Understand that this boss is all about self-gain and often may say one thing and do the opposite. Do not make the politician look bad, and make sure you let them know when something will be a problem for them politically. Do not talk publicly about this person in a negative manner. Your job is to make them look good and to do so while maintaining honesty and without compromising your values, integrity, and character.

Incompetent Boss

You are a threat to this person, and so is everyone else. Be very careful with this boss. They cannot do the job, everyone can see it, but for some reason they are in charge of you and perhaps your department. Protect yourself. Document what you do, your meetings and discussions, and save the information.

If you are able to develop a relationship so that they are willing to accept help from you, you may be able to help them. However, if they have been in the business for a while, it may be a lost cause.

Motivational Boss

When you are working for this boss, you should be motivated to work harder and more enthusiastically. Keep up the good energy, and you will feed off each other. Do not complain or show signs of pessimism.

Stressed-Out Boss

This boss can cause a very difficult and high-stress atmosphere for everyone. Often, workers are afraid to do anything because they are not sure what will cause the boss to go off. Try to stay below the radar and do your job. Do not take it to heart when you are yelled at. Do not react to their tantrum—reacting only feeds it. Remain professional at all times.

Get to know your boss. Find out what they think is funny and what is important to them. The more you get to know this individual, the better chance you have of diffusing the attack. Sometimes the unexpected throws them off guard and stops the tantrum. While I do not recommend this action, one time I was on the other side of a tantrum from a stressed-out boss, one I had known for years. As she was screaming at me, I walked up to her and gave her a hug. She broke out laughing, tantrum over. I could do that only because we had known each other for many years and we were in a public area.

Each stressed-out boss has different triggers, so you will need different tactics to diffuse the anger. Often, it is a joke. However, you may not be the one who has the control. If you do not have a close relationship with this boss, you should be very cautious.

The Nuclear Reactor

The nuclear reactor has some similarities to the stressed-out boss, and the atmosphere might be similar. Again, staying below the radar and just doing your job is usually the right step in a negative environment.

Timing can be very important with this boss. You do not want to give the reactive boss bad news right after a nuclear meltdown. If you need to give them bad news, give them the news at a time when you can avoid the explosion. This person should come back to their senses, given time.

When delivering something that could cause a meltdown, try to give them a time frame for reacting later—perhaps letting them know that you do not need a decision for a week.

Absent Boss

The most difficult challenge with this leader is pinning down the absentee and actually getting answers. If you need guidance, direction, or a decision before you can move forward, the boss's absence will slow down your process.

Emails can be very helpful in covering your actions and identifying all your attempts to talk or see this person. But depending on your situation, sometimes you may have to make a decision to move forward. If you are dealing with deadlines, you may not have a choice—the boss is not there, and the work must get done. There may not even be a post-decision discussion with the absent boss, simply because they are still not around. The worst-case scenario might be a reprimand, a suspension, or even getting fired for moving forward without the boss's stamp of approval. You need to know your situation to make the decision that is best for you and your institution.

While email can be helpful for documenting your efforts, it is not the same as developing a relationship with the boss. Try to get to know this individual and establish a relationship. Make the most of the time when this boss is around.

Substance-Abusing Boss

This boss has multiple issues that could put you in some difficult situations. The most important thing is for you to do your job and to monitor the daily situation. Every day can be a new experience, depending on the situation. If there is a process that would allow you to get this person professional help, it can be the best for everyone.

However, this category is often combined with other categories. Document everything you see and your dealings with this person to protect yourself—you will never know when documentation might be needed in the future. If there is someone you trust who is on the same level as your boss or above, you may want to give them a heads-up. But be aware that this could backfire if the person turns out not to be trustworthy or is a weak administrator.

Average Everyday Boss

By definition, this is the kind of boss most of us are dealing with. If you have the average boss, being a good worker goes a long way. They may not be flamboyant or emotional, but they may have been in the position awhile and be fairly well respected. Do not underestimate their ability or power.

I have always said there are two kinds of power. The first is the power you get with your title, which is what the "power boss" depends on, but the other is the power you earn over time in a position. Longevity power is actually stronger because it comes from the respect of employees. Everyone needs to do their part for this team. As long as you are doing your part, you should be all right with your average everyday leader.

Insecure Boss

This boss is very insecure about their ability to get people to follow them. Therefore, they feel threatened by the successful people around them. Being humble might help, but if you are good at what you do, you will have a good reputation, and any honors you receive will be like putting salt on the boss's wound. Typically this manager will try to get rid of anyone who is good at what they do, or at least good enough that they seem like a threat in this manager's mind.

If you are known for your expertise, try to stay under the radar and build your boss's confidence by offering positive feedback when possible. It can be difficult if you are experienced, because the better you do your job, the worse the boss's insecurity becomes. However, you do not want to lessen what you do, since scaling back your efforts will likely hurt your employer's business.

If this boss has someone above them who is astute, then eventually upper management may see that some of the best people are leaving or being forced out or fired.

The Hitman or Hitwoman

If you have been identified as a target, start documenting everything—a good practice for your own protection in any situation. Always be cautious when dealing with this manager. Do not believe what they say, and be aware that you are going to be set up, especially if you are good at what you do.

There are three ways this person will try to oust their target. The first is to try to show that the target is incompetent. If that is not possible, then they may try to make you *look* incompetent. They will not give you any support and make it hard for you to succeed. Finally, if all else fails, they may set you up to take the blame for something they caused. In this case, you will need to defend yourself at some point. You may even need to take on this manager head-to-head. The more information you have to protect yourself and perhaps hurt this person if your back is against the wall, the better.

If you are not the target, watch and learn, because no one knows who is next. Start documenting. Keep anything you dig up on this person or give it to the person who is the current target, providing the target is actually good for the institution and profession.

The Manipulator

Communication with this boss should be very clear, and have your communication witnessed by others or recorded, for example in an email. Copy others on emails. The more people who witness the communication, the less manipulating can be done. The manipulator is not always vicious—a good manipulator can do it in such a subtle way that people are not even aware it is being done.

It can be argued that motivation techniques are a form of manipulation, so this type of manager is not always bad. Some people are natural manipulators, and there are benefits to having these skills. But there is a fine line, and once it is crossed, things start falling apart for this manager. Just understanding how this person operates will help you navigate and know when it is important to make sure everyone understands exactly what you are saying.

Family Boss

If you are part of a family business, understand the family values and each individual you have to deal with. Place a high priority on making the family business successful. If you are part of the family, try to have boundaries. What is at work stays at work. Living with your family can be hard enough, but then working with them makes things even more challenging. I worked in the family business for years, and I do not remember ever talking about business during our personal time, except for maybe what the plans were the next day or what time we had to meet somewhere.

If you are not a member of the family, it is important to understand the power structure. As an outsider, often you may not have the support family members have. This can be frustrating for outsiders, especially if one of the family members is not very good at the job. Never do or say anything against the family, the family business, or individuals of the family. Do your job, and eventually you may earn the respect needed to have more job security. I have seen some workers earn a great deal of respect and even become almost an equal to family members. However, family connections are deep, and if you cross a line, you will see how strong the family relationships are.

Because there is a direct line to the personal life of everyone in the business, work can be very challenging during a family crisis. I believe the hardest work day in my life was when my father left my mother on my graduation day, and on the following day I had to report to work with my father. Everything changed overnight, and there were a lot of emotions, especially anger toward my father. I was very quiet that day and probably for weeks after. I knew my father and brother were feeling the awkwardness as well. However, it was work and personal things were not discussed.

I was very fortunate to have a family business in my life that taught me work values and was the basis of my career in many ways. I always wanted to have a family business so that my children could learn those values as well, but as it turned out, my chosen career did not involve the family business.

The Best Friend

The boss who wants to be your best friend can be a challenge if you do not want that type of relationship or you already have a best friend. Draw your line in a tactful manner. If you hurt the feelings of this individual, it can cause problems for you. Be friendly, courteous, and cordial, but tactful. Do not cross any lines that you do not want to cross. Do your job well, but understand that this person's desire to gain a friend could mean your job, especially in a small business.

The Social Media Boss

Social media bosses are all about controlling social media. To be on their good side, you may also want go on to social media. Depending on your profession, being on social media can be a positive or a negative. I have seen many people lose their jobs due to social media issues. You may have to make that decision if asked or directed to go on to social media.

Understand what you see on social media from this person is all about painting a picture that this boss wants people to perceive. It is not necessarily accurate, but it can make people think it is. This boss is usually about building their support, so as long as you are not a contradiction to that, you should be okay to go about your business by doing your job.

Interim Boss

Since this boss is not planning on staying in this position for whatever reason, usually if you do your job, there will not be any interference. However, it depends on the particular circumstances that makes this boss "interim." This boss could be combined with other categories, which would have an effect on the workers under this manager. For example, sometimes positions are filled with an interim boss who is also a hitman or hitwoman. The interim hitman or hitwoman is trying to clean out so-called undesirables from the workplace so that the boss has a great team to lead immediately upon arrival. Or the interim boss could be in the position just to kill time until the new boss prepares for arrival.

Usually, an interim boss is not there to do anything other than to manage the daily operations of the business or institution. You will need to know the details and see what other categories this boss falls into to be able to navigate this manager appropriately.

In the next chapter, I will introduce the concept of the combination boss. There are many, many combination-boss possibilities. I will discuss how to identify a combination boss, and then give a few examples of specific combinations.

3

Combination Bosses

As outlined in chapter 1, a boss can fit into more than one category. In fact, there are too many combinations to cover all possible combinations in this book. Instead, this chapter will focus on identifying the multiple-category boss.

The boss you are dealing with may fit into multiple categories, but start with the category you see as the best fit. Then write down any characteristics you are seeing that do not fit into the category you first selected. Is there one characteristic that is more pronounced? Is there a pattern to when you are seeing the behavior? Then go back and review what category or categories best fit these behaviors. Once you have identified the multiple categories your boss fits into, review chapter 2 for the dos and don'ts for each type. Then it will be time to start developing an action plan, as described in chapter 4.

Let's look at three examples of the multicategory boss.

Micromanager/Power/Egotistical/Social Media

The combination of the micromanager, the power boss, the egotistical boss, and the social media boss can result in one who is masterful in painting a picture for people to see toward the self-gain of the boss. This boss does not rely on their expert employees but instead tries to control every aspect of everything possible, while refusing to be held accountable for anything that goes wrong even if they had micromanaged it. This boss will say one thing publicly but is likely to do something else behind the scenes. On social media, they will put out anything, true or false, as long as they think it will help their situation.

This boss will usually be able to get away with a lot because people are looking at a fabricated picture while the organization itself may very well be falling apart. The atmosphere may start off very positive, but as more and more people realize the truth, the support will lessen. As the support becomes less, the boss becomes more dangerous. Remember, this boss will say anything for their own gain. Often this boss believes they will need to take someone down to move forward.

What do you do when dealing with this combination? Remember, they need to be the center of attention (the egotistical boss) and will even paint a picture with fabricated material (the social media boss). Do not publicly humiliate this boss unless your back is against the wall and you feel you do not have any other choice. It is vital to keep all your factual information and records. Put as much as possible in writing about your viewpoints, the facts, and your predictions so that if or when you are blamed, you have the facts to show—this boss will likely blame someone if things do not go well.

The power boss part of this combination wants full control and will do anything to make your job more difficult and you as miserable as possible, especially if you are perceived as a threat or as someone who has a different point of view. Keeping your head held high and being positive will help you get through the day and will likely not make this boss happy. The power boss wants you to show a reaction of being mad, scared, or disappointed. Do not give this boss the satisfaction. Keep your immediate atmosphere as positive as possible, and the people around you will appreciate it and respect how strong you are. It is about your mental and physical health as well as what is best for the organization.

Incompetent/Hitman or Hitwoman

This combination can be both negative and positive. First, remember that this boss was hired to force out or fire at least one person. If you are not that person, then just go about your business working hard while studying what this boss does—it will be helpful if you are next on the list. The negative part of this person is that this boss does not have a mind of their own. They are not there to learn anything about the person they are targeting; they are there to achieve a mission. The positive part of this combination is that their incompetence means you are likely to know more than they do and possibly have better skills.

B O S S

If you believe you are your boss's target, do not believe anything they say and always have your guard up. Remember, they are looking to get you out. If the hitman or hitwoman cannot find any reason or factual evidence that you are doing a bad job, they will likely just make it up. Keep all your records and data, and save your memos and emails. Continue to do your job as best as you can, despite the challenges that will be thrown your way. This person's incompetence gives you the edge to win this battle.

True Leader/Motivational

If you are fortunate, you may come across the combination of the true leader and the motivational boss. This is a great combination. This type of boss may have people lining up to work for him or her.

If you have a motivational leader as a boss, keep in mind that they are all about moving the organization forward and at the same time moving each individual forward. This boss has high expectations and treats people well. You must be on top of your game and always trying to improve. Everyone is likely to be excited to be working for this boss. The atmosphere is energized, exciting, and positive, and the organization is likely doing well.

You can usually talk to this boss. If you have an issue, discuss it. Enjoy your time with this boss, because when it changes, this is the kind of boss you will miss. Learn from this leader. Watch how they treat people, how they run meetings, and how they handle a problem or a crisis. If you can learn from this boss, you are more likely to become a true leader or a motivator yourself.

4

Your Boss and Your Work Environment: Should You Stay or Go?

The work environment is arguably the most important aspect of any job. While the work environment very much results from the administration in charge, there are various factors that can affect the atmosphere.

- Does everyone enjoy working in this location?

- Are people positive about their experiences at this workplace?

- Are the goals of the organization being achieved?

- Do you see and feel the excitement in the organization?

- Is the atmosphere consistent and fair for all?

- Is the perception of the atmosphere the same for everyone, or is it different by department?

- If the boss leaves, will the environment change?

For this last question, sometimes you can get a feeling for the answer when the boss leaves for even a few hours. An environment that changes during the boss's absence may be confirmation that the boss is the root cause of your work environment.

Once you answer the questions above, ask yourself how long the atmosphere has been in place. We know that the atmosphere of the workplace starts at the top of the organization—the person in charge, perhaps the board or even a committee. Whatever the reason, the fact is that people leave or try to get into a workplace largely because its reputation as a good work environment.

It is important to understand that one book will not have all the answers, and there are always going to be variables not be covered here. But you can take the relevant information from this book and combine it with these other contributing factors. When you have to make a fight-or-flight decision, first you need to identify whether you are in an environment you want to be in, and how long you believe the environment will continue to be as it is.

Here are eight steps for making a decision and developing an action plan.

1. Identify and categorize the boss or bosses you are working for.

2. Review the dos and don'ts for interacting with your boss or bosses.

3. Identify your work environment and if it is where you want to work.

4. Try to figure out whether the workplace atmosphere is stable or possibly going to change.

5. If you decide to stay, develop a set of goals you want to achieve, perhaps three or four, while working under this boss.

6. Align your goals with the dos and don'ts for the boss or bosses you have.

7. Break down your goals into achievable steps, with a timeline for achieving each step.

8. List behaviors for working with each boss that can be used to achieve your goals.

Once you have completed these steps, you can start implementing your plan. At each step, review your actions and their outcomes in relation to the category or categories you put your boss or bosses in. Regularly evaluate whether your plan is working and then make adjustments as needed.

You should also reevaluate your boss as you carry out your plan. Remember, bosses can change over time. Would you still put this boss in the same category now as when you started? Have they developed and grown or improved? This is especially important if your plan is to be carried out over a long period of time. Hopefully, you can be an asset to your boss in their own development toward becoming a more productive boss for the organization.

5

Becoming a Boss

Being a leader is not for everyone. You must want to be the person in charge. You should have good character, integrity, and a positive attitude. It is helpful if you have a mission in life that corresponds to being a boss. My life goal has and will always be to help others. Everything I've done in my life has evolved around that mission, and that particular mission goes well with being a boss. I have found that the higher I have gone in an organization, the more people I can help. I went from helping small groups of five to thirty people to helping many thousands of people over time.

So if you decide to take the path of being a boss, here are a few tips from someone who has been in charge almost all his life.

- Always remember that you are never done learning, and those who work for you must have the opportunity to learn as well.

- Remember that people respond to positive communication. I recommend the 80/20 rule. Make 80 percent of your communications positive. Then people will actually hear the 20 percent that are criticisms.

- Be honest. People respect those who are honest, even if they do not want to hear what you have to say.

- Accept accountability for your actions. Nothing loses respect faster than a boss who is not accountable.

- Pick the category you want to be in this book, or perhaps a couple of categories, then set out a plan for achieving that goal.

- Take on leadership roles as often as possible.

- Be humble.

- Get to know the people in your organization, and observe how they react to things that happen in the workplace.

- Ask yourself if you would have done what that boss did, or if there was another way.

- Learn from your boss. No matter how good or bad a boss is, you can learn a lot from their actions. While from some you will learn what you should do, from others you will learn a great deal on what *not* to do.

- Read. There are countless books dealing with leadership, motivation, organization, and professionalism. The more you read, the more you learn.

- Take courses on leadership, either generally or within your area in the workforce.

- Get involved in your profession by going to workshops and conferences and joining committees. Develop your professional image, but please, make it real: eventually people see through a fake persona.

- Enjoy your work each and every day as best as you can.

6

The Social Styles Approach and Your Boss Type

Have you figured out which category or categories your boss fits into? Knowing and understanding the type of boss you are dealing with is a step in the right direction. Now it is time to start looking at the individual as well.

Over the years, I have used something known as "social styles" to help me learn how to deal with bosses as well as colleagues. It can even be more helpful to figure out what your social style is and what type of boss you would like to be.

In the late 1990s, I attended a professional conference where we were introduced to the idea of social styles and asked to identify our own style. Once each of us had identified our own social style, the presenter asked us to move to one of the corners of the room as designated by style. To the shock of everyone in the room, every person but two crammed into a single corner of the room, including me. It was funny to everyone at the time. However, it created a couple of questions for me. First, was everyone this style before taking on the job they were in? Or is it the job itself that develops the style?

I have concluded from my experience over the years that styles are developed over time and do change in relation to your position and experience. I believe your style is a mixture of personality, experience, and the expectations of the position.

I gathered this material originally from the workshop I attended and later from the book *People Styles at Work* by R. Bolton and D. Bolton. While this book has aged, the material is still very helpful. I don't want to go over this material in great depth, but understanding social styles along with your boss's category can benefit you in your quest to understand your boss.

The Boltons place people into four distinct basic styles: *driver, analytical, amiable,* and *expressive.* These were the four styles we were asked at the conference to "corner" ourselves into. The people who gathered in my corner of the room had chosen driver as their style.

The **driver** is a go-getter. They are often great for lower management positions because they are the people who get things done. They are fast-moving, goal-oriented individuals. They can be viewed as sometimes being too pushy and tough, but they will achieve their goals.

The **analytic** is a person who has an objective sense of what is happening. Such a person is organized, reviews all the facts and information before making decisions, and is sometimes seen as rigid and even indecisive. The analytic will usually delegate responsibilities.

The **amiable** person is the emotional one of the styles. However, they may not express their emotions and are somewhat quiet. This person will take everything you say to heart. They are loyal and empathetic individuals who do not move too fast. They avoid conflict and can be very supportive of others.

The last group is the **expressive**. This group is seen as dramatic, enthusiastic, and creative. They are also often viewed as being too excitable and undisciplined. They express their feelings whether you are ready for it or not. They are driven by impulse, and their energy level can be contagious.

So the question is how to relate the category of your boss to their social style type. The Boltons' book has a questionnaire to help you identify your style, but you cannot ask your boss to take a test. So let's go over a few questions with examples that may help you identify the style of your boss.

If your boss sees something you know they are not happy with, how do they act?

- The **driver** may point it out and correct immediately, thus taking control of the situation.

- The **analytic** may observe and ponder the situation and then talk to the person for corrective action.

- The **amiable** may see and feel for those who might have been affected in a negative manner.

- The **expressive** might blow up and become dramatic about the incident.

When you watch the boss go about a normal day, how do they frame their time?

- If they are moving quickly and trying to handle the immediate emergencies of the day, they are probably a **driver**.

- The **analytical** will be moving at a slower pace and reviewing or observing what has happened.

- The **amiable** will be moving much slower, concerned with what is happening and smoothing everything out as it happens.

- The **expressive** will be in the moment in terms of all eyes on them, bringing the energy to the room, good or bad. They move quickly and react quickly. You always know how this person is feeling—their whole body lets you know, as well as their verbal expression.

Have you seen the boss in a stressful situation?

- The **driver** will take it on as another goal or obstacle to defeat.

- The **analytic** may try to avoid the situation.

- The **amiable** will take the easiest route, even if it means giving into something they may not want to do.

- The **expressive** will attack like a tiger, possibly saying things they do not mean or causing an incident that could be viewed as uncalled for.

Have you been able to identify where your boss fits in? How do you use the information gained from identifying the category or categories of your boss along with social style? Look back at chapter 2 on the dos and the don'ts of your boss and chapter 4 on developing your action plan. How does social style fit into that?

7

Making Time for Yourself

The final chapter of this book is designed to remind you to take care of yourself. Bad bosses can increase the chance of a stroke by 33 percent, according to Tom Rath and Donald O. Clifton in *How Full Is Your Bucket?* At the same time, increasing positive emotions could lengthen your lifespan by ten years. Filling your bucket increases productivity and lifespan, and will make you a better boss or worker.

Moving to a position with a higher level of responsibilities often increases your stress and the amount of time you have to commit to work. Your life becomes more of an open book, and it is common for a boss to be criticized publicly or at least within the organization. Everyone has an opinion. For the sake of your productivity and health, you must take care of yourself by "filling your bucket," both at work and by making the best of your time when you are away from work. Plan activities for outside work as part of your day. Something as simple as having lunch out can be a relief.

Taking care of yourself is not always going to be easy. Try to make the best of time away from work. If you become a boss, remember that the burden placed on you will also fall on those closest to you. More time at work means less time with your family and friends. The stress you are dealing with, can overflow to those closest to you. Eat right, be active, and exercise as needed. Make sure you have regular checkups with your physician— especially when you are in a stressful situation or position of responsibility. Do things you enjoy. Keep your interactions with others positive. Doing that will help keep your bucket filled as well as helping others keep their bucket filled.

Finally, when you have a bad day and feel stressed, do something that reminds you of the good things your institution is doing. Go out and take a walk. Look at the final product that is produced by your work, whatever that is. Look at the good things going on in your building or organization and understand that you are a big part of that.

From the viewpoint of one ordinary person, I hope that this book helps you in dealing with a difficult boss, making a decision about a job, or becoming a boss who is trying to become the best you can.

About the Author

jameswrose.com

James Rose is an educational professional and a graduate of SUNY College at Cortland, where he studied physical education, and of Columbia University, Teachers College, where he furthered his knowledge about educational administration. He is a respected professional, teacher, coach, author, leader, administrator, presenter, consultant, and expert witness, who has received many leadership awards over the years. He has worked for more than fifty bosses during thirty-five years as a professional and for many other bosses during summers and holding jobs during his younger years. Along the way, he has learned both positive and negative attributes of leadership which have molded his own administrative style. He has supervised thousands of employees over the years and has held many leadership positions to further the profession of education.

James Rose has been an active volunteer emergency medical technician and firefighter for over forty years. His lifelong mission is to help others. As part of that mission, he hopes this book can assist the worker who works very hard every day but struggles with a particular boss, or all those who are looking for insight into understanding the people within a workplace or the type of boss they may want to become. James has a family of four with two sons.

Printed in the United States
by Baker & Taylor Publisher Services